SHORTCUT TO SUCCESS

WTT | WEB TENNIS TRAINING

MAXIMIZE YOUR TENNIS POTENTIAL

SHORTCUT TO SUCCESS

Author: **RIHARDS EMULINS**

FOLLOW US:

www.webtennistraining.com

facebook.com/webtennistraining

instagram.com/webtennistraining

youtube.com/webtennistraining

twitter.com/webtenniscoach

SHORTCUT TO SUCCESS

ISBN 978-9934-23-004-2

IN TENNIS YOU HAVE TO BELIEVE THAT YOU CAN BEAT ANYBODY.

YES, ANYBODY!

TIPS, DRILLS, STRATEGIES AND MINDSET FOR WINNING TENNIS.

TABLE OF CONTENTS

INTRODUCTION	7
GOOD TECHNIQUE MAKES LIFE EASIER	31
BEING FIT IS IMPORTANT	49
THE BRAIN GAME	69
IT IS ALL IN YOUR MIND	101

INTRODUCTION

SUCCESS IN LIFE IS CLOSER THAN YOU THINK!

It is all about a journey not a destination. It is all about an ability to enjoy the process. Success is a continuous improvement, in order to maximize your potential and become the best you can be.

The same applies to tennis. Of course, winning Grand Slams, being famous and making millions is a success as well. It is a dream for every tennis player. However, we all are different. We all have different stories, different backgrounds and different possibilities. For someone only winning a Grand Slam counts as a success. But, at the same time, someone else dreams about winning a match in a local club. Success is all about improving and maximizing your own potential.

When I learnt this simple lesson, I stopped comparing myself to others. I started to focus on my own journey and my tennis results improved immensely. I won National championship, represented my country in Davis Cup and achieved ATP ranking point. I know that it is quite far from winning a Grand Slam, but I feel good about myself. I will never stop improving, however I feel that I'm close to maximizing my potential.

I still compete from time to time, but I'm a tennis coach now. And I'm willing to share with you my experience and things I have learnt in my journey so far, so that you don't need to go through the same struggles I went through. I'm offering you a shortcut to success.

LET'S DIVE IN!

TENNIS IS LIFE

SPORT IS TOUGH. PHYSICALLY AND MENTALLY.
EMBRACE IT! ENJOY IT!
BECAUSE SPORT IS BEAUTIFUL.

One of the greatest tennis players of all time Andre Agassi once said: "It's no accident, I think, that tennis uses the language of life. Advantage, service, fault, break, love, the basic elements of tennis are those of everyday existence, because every match is a life in miniature. Even the structure of tennis, the way the pieces fit inside one another like Russian nesting dolls, mimics the structure of our days. Points become games become sets become tournaments, and it's all so tightly connected that any point can become the turning point. It reminds me of the way seconds become minutes become hours, and any hour can be our finest. Or darkest. It's our choice."

Tennis has given me a lot. There have been so many positive emotions after every win and so many tough lessons learnt after every loss. Every practice session has made me a better tennis player and strengthened my character. Every injury, every missed flight and every night spent in my car while traveling to tournaments have made me more patient.

Every point in every match has given me a task to solve. And I still enjoy solving those tasks.

YOU AGAINST YOURSELF

YOU AGAINST YOURSELF… THAT IS THE BIGGEST BATTLE YOU MUST WIN, IF YOU WANT TO BE SUCCESSFUL IN TENNIS.

Rafael Nadal's uncle and coach, Toni, once said:
"Success is not winning Roland Garros or US Open. Success is improving. Winning a Grand Slam does not depend only on me, but also on my opponents. I have to worry about what depends on me and what I can improve on. That is a success."

Very often your opponent isn't your biggest problem, but your own mind is. Ability to practice hard and push yourself, staying positive, not giving up, not doubting, not thinking about your opponent too much, trusting instincts and sticking to the game plan… These are must do things, if you want to have a success in tennis. And it doesn't really matter what is your level of play. If you can serve, rally and count the score, these things apply to you.

Imagine the morning before you are going to play an important tennis match. You know that you have practiced tennis regularly and worked on your fitness as well, and you really enjoy tennis, but… You are nervous. Big time nervous! Or even scared to extent that you don't want to eat, your arms are shaking, and your state of mind is far away from being ready for a competitive tennis match.

Most of the tennis players of different levels have experienced some sort of anxiety before a tennis match. So... Have you ever doubted yourself before a tennis match? Have you ever thought that the opponent you are going to face is too tough to beat? And let me guess... You lost that match? Or maybe there have been match when you were too confident going in? And as the match progressed the result wasn't going in your favor and in the end you lost to, as you thought, "weaker" opponent. Have you ever stepped on the tennis court for competitive match without a clear game plan? Or have you ever let different distractions in your mind take you away from your game plan even if you had one? Or maybe there has been a match when you were over prepared and created several game plans, but got confused in your tactical decisions by jumping from one plan to another thus letting unnecessary errors creep in your game? Or maybe even worse... You are a recreational player, practice regularly a few times per week for many years and you have learnt all technical stuff necessary for competing against other players, and you are physically fit, but... You just can't imagine yourself getting out on the match court and playing a competitive tennis match. You enjoy tennis as a sport, however even the idea about competing makes you nervous and you better decide that it is not for you...

No worries

WE ALL HAVE BEEN THERE BECAUSE WE ARE HUMAN BEINGS WITH MIND AND EMOTIONS.

And the key is to find the right balance between mind and emotions. And to find that balance we need knowledge. And that is what I'm going to share with you from my personal experience as a player and as a coach. I will share with you everything I have learnt in tennis so that you don't need to go through the same struggles I went through for decades trying to figure out a beautiful game of tennis. So, in this book I will offer you a shortcut to success. And mostly I will be talking about singles. However, remember that it is just an information. You will have to put it in the practice yourself.

I'm a big believer that competition makes us better. I think that without competition there is no progress and practicing become pointless in any level. Competition motivates us to practice harder and helps in setting goals we want to achieve. Only in competition we can really asses our level and see things we need to work on in our practice sessions. And it isn't all about the result. We should focus on the process and learn to asses our performance. Winning or losing is secondary. We can't really control it. Not being afraid, going out there to compete and giving your all is what matters. Just focus on the process and believe that the result will eventually come, if you do all the right things.

Actually, writing this book helped my own tennis career. By writing it, I reminded myself to focus on the process more and not to think about the result so much. I started to respect myself and enjoy tennis more than before. When I started writing this book, I wasn't quite happy about what I have achieved in tennis. In a way, I even hated myself for not being able to accomplish one of my biggest tennis goals – to achieve ATP ranking. ATP ranking is a big deal for any tennis player. Even the world's best tennis players still recall getting that first professional ranking point as one of their greatest tennis memories. And it is totally understandable because it is really difficult to become a true professional. There used to be only approximately 2000 male players in ATP ranking and a little bit fewer female players in WTA ranking.

Tennis is an incredibly popular sport. In fact, it is one of the most popular sports in the world with more than a billion followers. Approximately hundred million people play tennis worldwide and more than ten thousand players are competing in professional tennis tournaments every year. So, the competition is immense and being among those two thousand men who have these prestigious ATP ranking points seemed a big deal to me.

It took me 13 years to achieve my goal and get that one ATP singles ranking point. I was 16 years old when I played my first professional tennis tournament and I was 29 when I got my first ATP ranking point.

It took some time, didn't it? And the funniest thing is that I finally achieved my goal while I was half way through writing this book. Putting my thoughts together and writing them all down on paper helped me to become mentally tougher and my head became clearer. And I truly believe that this information can help you to achieve your goals as well.

My tennis story

THE BEGINNING OF MY TENNIS CARRER
WAS PRETTY HUMBLE.

My name is Rihards Emulins. I was born in 1987, in Latvia, and started playing tennis back in 1994 when I was 7 years old. I was a part of large group of children with different age and tennis abilities. I call it a "health group" where children were mainly sent for just having fun and play some sport twice per week. There were no professional goals and I, and my family had no idea what professional tennis means. Luckily, my parents both were professional athletes and I want to thank them for everything they have done for me. Actually, I want to thank my whole family. They are awesome!

Alright! Back to the point… My mother Inga was a national champion and a member of Soviet Union team in artistic gymnastics. My father Raimonds was a national champion and the captain of Latvian national handball team. So, I turned out to be an active kid. I played different sports whenever I could and every evening I went with my father to his handball practices. I loved sport from the very beginning. However, tennis came as a lucky coincidence. My mother didn't want me to play handball as it is a very rough sport and tennis court (yes, one court in the hotel not a massive tennis club) was really close to my school. That was the only reason I picked up a tennis racket. Good for me that I didn't become artistic gymnast...

I spent next 5 years in that "health group" where often we were 6 or even more players on a single tennis court. With that little amount of training and so many players on court it is almost impossible for a coach to teach decent fundamentals. So, you can imagine how weird looking technique (wrong grips, lack of shoulder turn, etc.) I had, and my tactical knowledge of tennis was poor. However, my first coach Diana Radionova did a great job of making those short tennis sessions exciting and very competitive. I also noticed that I was pretty strong physically and I felt that I had a will to be successful. But success didn't come easy and it took a lot of time.

I was 12 years old when I became more serious about tennis. School and education were still a priority for me. But I started practicing in a bigger tennis club with better players and my new coach Maris Rozentals was a great role model. At the time he was already 40 years old, but he was able to beat some of the best Latvian juniors who were more than two times younger than him. He was really inspirational and motivated me to compete more. So, I started competing more often in local tournaments. I was an average tennis player even for a national standard. Definitely, closer to the bottom than the top end. I improved a little bit as I practiced more and became physically stronger. I had a really good fitness coach Alberts Baturins. We worked together for almost a decade. Fitness sessions with him made me stronger not only physically, but also mentally. Training was extremely difficult as Alberts used to be a professional sprinter and also a bobsledder. And if you have seen a movie about a boxer called Rocky Balboa, then something similar happened in my fitness training with Alberts. I was running sprints on the beach in the winter while it was snowing. I was dragging heavy truck tires in the forest on early Sunday morning and I was doing dozens of pull ups just for a warm up. It was a great time and all those years of heavy physical training gave me a good foundation for my whole tennis career. However, my stroke technique and tactical awareness on the tennis court remained pretty much at the same level.

Then, three years later, things got more serious. I was 15 years old when I started to train with a really experienced tennis coach Pauls Feldmanis, who had a huge international experience including traveling with ATP World Tour level players. I spent there three great years and my technique got much better. I finally practiced tennis every day. In addition to group training I finally had individual training as well. We did a lot of live drills, basket drills and point play. I was finally practicing as a professional and I got better. My grips were finally fixed, I started using more shoulder rotation during my strokes and my footwork became more fluent. However, I still wasn't passionate for tennis. I liked practicing and competing, but I wasn't putting enough thoughts into the tennis. I was completely focused when I was on the court. I was fighting like crazy during my matches. I was sometimes even having cramps in my legs and in my arms, but I never gave up and I always kept on fighting. I enjoyed winning and hated losing, but I kind of forgot about tennis when I was off the court. I liked tennis and I wanted to be successful, but I wasn't truly in love with it…

I was 18 years old when I started to fell in love with tennis. I was about to graduate from the high school. That is the time when you have to take more responsibility about your own life and you can't depend solely on your parents' financial help. So, I started coaching. I coached players of different levels and ages. And by starting coaching, I started exploring tennis in a more detailed way. And, eventually, I started understanding my own game better. My tennis IQ grew, and I tested everything I taught on myself. I also spoke with other coaches, studied, attended seminars and conferences, watched tennis on TV more than ever, as well as learnt on the Internet. I slowly became obsessed with tennis.

I was coaching, but also kept practicing and competing myself. I won national junior championship and became a member of Latvian national junior team, so I got a few free practice sessions per week. I also practiced alone with the ball machine and my father helped me a lot. It was difficult, but really nice time. I had to squeeze in my own practice sessions in my schedule, which was stuffed with lectures in the university and coaching. So very often I started my training with the ball machine even before 8 a.m. Very often my father was there as well and our effort paid off. At the age of 20 I won Latvian national championship and made a debut in Latvian Davis Cup team in a tie against Bulgaria. Our team won, however I lost my singles match 2:6 5:7. I didn't capitalize on two set points in the second set. Ouch! But it was an awesome experience anyway. And I wanted more. I wanted to play in a professional level and achieve ATP ranking. I was already 20 years old and I knew that it is pretty late to set such goals as it is great to know what you want to achieve in tennis by the age of 10... But as an old saying goes: ''Better later than never!''

I kept studying, coaching and developing my own game. The schedule was difficult and my days began at 6 a.m. and ended around midnight after all my university work was done. But I enjoyed that. The only problem was that in my country and in my region there were just a few professional tournaments per year. And as you can imagine travelling was expensive. Moreover, it was also tough to combine travelling with the university. But I had a plan. I got my bachelor's degree in business administration in Latvia and moved to Scotland to get my master's degree and keep playing tennis. I got a tennis scholarship in the University of Stirling, which is one of the best universities of sports sciences in the United Kingdom.

And then came my biggest breakthrough. Those two years I spent in Scotland were amazing. I not only got my master's degree in sports management, but also tremendously improved my tennis. At the age of 23, I finally had well-structured practice plan and regularly scheduled tournaments. I practiced tennis twice almost every day and worked on my fitness on daily basis. I had competitive matches and tournaments almost every week. Tennis was finally my priority and I enjoyed the process so much.

I was finally able to beat professional full-time tennis players on a regular basis. In my career I have had several close matches with players ranked in ATP top 300. I have beaten a few players who were ranked around 500 in ATP ranking and I have had many important victories against a little bit lower ranked ATP players.

In my second year in Stirling University we won BUCS (British Universities and Colleges Sports) team championship. It is still one of the greatest moments of my tennis career. College taught me that tennis can actually be a team sport when you care about the results of other people as well. I had great team mates pushing me to become a better player and an awesome coaching staff. Our coach Euan McGinn helped me a lot, especially, by developing my doubles game. He taught me that doubles are won by being aggressive and playing at the net not by grinding from the baseline. In fact, me and my partner Joe Gill won doubles title in BUCS individual championship, which is one of my career highlights as well.

Our training facilities were in the Scottish National Tennis Centre where majority of the Scotland's best players and coaches were working together on daily basis. And I had a privilege to learn from Judy Murray, who is the mother of a Grand Slam singles champion Andy Murray and doubles champion Jamie Murray. She was coaching Scotland's best junior tennis players and I was often invited as a hitting partner in those practice sessions. I learnt a lot of valuable lessons from her.

Going to Stirling University to study and play tennis was one of my best decisions I have ever made. In fact, I believe that going to college as a tennis scholar is the best career option for the most of the young tennis players graduating from a high school. Unless a young player is among the world's best junior players and is already showing good results in a professional tennis, it is a great idea to go to the college. Firstly, it provides you an opportunity to get a degree. Secondly, you get an incredible life experience and mature not only as a tennis player, but also as a person. Thirdly, you can seriously improve your tennis and try to become a professional after graduating from a college. Many current ATP and WTA players have done it. For example, John Isner, Steve Johnson, Danielle Collins and many other great players have graduated form a college before starting their professional tennis careers. And it doesn't matter you go to USA, Great Britain or any other country offering sports scholarships. College tennis is awesome everywhere as it provides a great platform for combining studying, training and competing.

I graduated from the University of Stirling at the age of 25 by playing the best tennis of my life. However, professional sport is taxing on the body and over the years of grinding, I picked up a chronic wrist injury, which seriously limited my ability to play full time professional tennis. So, I went back home to Latvia and helped my sister Darta Elizabete Emulina in her tennis career. During our work together, she won Latvian national junior championship, competed in a professional circuit for many years and at the age of 16 made a debut in Latvian Fed Cup team. By the way, she still plays a decent tennis and we often practice together.

Despite my injury, I haven't given up and still compete from time to time. When I'm writing these lines, I just turned 30 and I'm recovering from the surgery on my injured wrist. I hope to be back on the match court soon and compete as I did in previous years. At the age of 27, I was able to reach the final of ITF Futures doubles tournament in Latvia with my partner Krisjanis Stabins. And, as I already told you, at the age of 29 I made a debut in ATP singles ranking by winning a first round in the main draw in ITF Futures tournament in Estonia.

TENNIS IS SOMETHING I KNOW THE BEST AND I CAN TALK ABOUT THIS SPORT ENDLESSLY.

As I said before, I make a living as a tennis coach. I teach both – online and also in the real life. The biggest part of my day is spent either on the tennis court playing or in front of the computer screen creating digital content. I have been very lucky to coach so many great people. The youngest person I have ever coached was 5 years old and the oldest, definitely, in 60+ age group. I have worked with complete beginners and eager recreational players. I have coached tireless kids and aspiring juniors. I have helped many young players to achieve their dream and receive scholarships for studying and playing college tennis. I have also worked with professional tennis players trying to reach the top of the game, so I have gained some experience.

In these 100 pages I have squeezed in pretty much everything I know about tennis. Well… Maybe not everything, but the main things for sure. And my training methods have helped thousands of players to take their games to the next level by following simple rules. And I hope they will help you as well.

This book is divided into 4 main chapters focusing on:

- Technique;
- Fitness;
- Strategy;
- Psychology.

LET'S BEGIN WITH TECHNIQUE!

GOOD TECHNIQUE MAKES LIFE EASIER

MOST OF THE TENNIS PLAYERS ARE TRYING TO BE PERFECT. MAYBE EVEN TOO PERFECT...

Having a good technique is important. But it is not all about technique. Look at Daniil Medvedev, for example. He is a great player, but his technique is not traditional and it is not perfect. However, he has many other top qualities, such as amazing fitness, outstanding decision making and strong mentality.

Even recreational tennis players come to every practice session with a vision that they will never miss again and all their strokes will finally be technically sound and clean. And guess what happens? They miss and get frustrated over and over again...

Of course, we should strive to become better, however we shouldn't be too harsh on ourselves and beat ourselves down, if we miss from time to time or our shots are not perfectly clean. Every shot in tennis requires so much precision that it is almost impossible to be perfect all the time. Even the world's best tennis players, who spend enormous amount of hours practicing, admit that many of their shots are not perfect. For example, former world number one and US Open champion Andy Roddick once said in the interview that most of his groundstrokes were not as perfect as he would like them to be. But he didn't panic about it. He kept working and enjoying the process of getting better.

Your technique doesn't have to be perfect, in order to hit with power and accuracy. Tennis is a game and it also includes fitness, strategy and psychology.

Technique, definitely, is the most important aspect of tennis. It is the first thing I notice when I see someone playing. Technique differs tennis players and their level of play. By having a good technique, tennis players can make their lives much easier not only game wise, but also health wise. By hitting a tennis ball in a wrong way, most likely it will lose speed, accuracy and human body will go through unnecessary physical stress thus causing fatigue and injuries.

Of course, basic fundamentals such as proper grip, shoulder turn, swing path, racket drop, follow through, footwork and other stuff must be right, however too many tennis players of different levels tend to forget that tennis is a game and they get stuck in perfecting their technique for too long, even if their technique already is good enough.

I have seen too many players, especially, recreational players who spend thousands of hours and thousands of dollars in perfecting their technique (most of the time forehand or backhand) with their coaches.

And when I ask about their next tournament or match, their typical answer is something like this: "I don't know... Well... My backhand... It is too slow... I have to practice more and compete later at some point... Those guys in the tournaments hit so hard..." Or some players, when asked how did their matches go last weekend, after losing very often say: "I lost. I must hit harder. Those guys hit so hard."

I had one student, solid gentleman, in his mid-forties who often competed in different recreational tournaments. I worked with him once per week and back in a day he was also suffering from "I want to hit harder" obsession. When I started coaching him, he blamed his technique after every loss. And even after every win... Then I decided to go and see one of his matches. He lost! To be honest, his opponent was hitting harder, however, that wasn't the reason he lost. My student made twice as many unforced errors as his opponent, including missed overheads, mid-court forehand errors, double faults and unnecessary drop shots in the net. And guess what... His excuse was: "The guy was hitting harder. Let's go and work on my technique! I want to hit as hard as he is hitting!" And then we started our long journey of learning that strokes in tennis are not about pure power. There is also placement, spin, trajectory and timing. All these factors are as important as power. What happens when Roger Federer plays against Rafael Nadal? Who hits flatter with more power? Of course, Federer! But who has won significantly more matches, when they face each other? Nadal! And there are many more similar examples, where power doesn't determine the winner.

I'm not saying that tennis players shouldn't work on their technique or hit hard. As I said before, I think that the technique is the most important aspect of tennis. For example, if you have a big technical weakness, then you should work on it and get it right. But notice that I said ''big weakness''. By big technical weakness I mean particular shot you are making a lot off unforced errors with. Slow second serve or short backhand is not a big weakness. Yes, it is a weakness, but not a major one. It needs to be improved, but you can still play with it and beat a lot of opponents who have better technique and more fluent strokes.

If you are able to hit the ball in the court, place it wherever you want and add some spin, you are ready to compete and win matches.

When you see a player with beautiful shot mechanics, you should also pay attention where he or she send those balls. Shots may be powerful, but do these hard-hit balls land inside the tennis court all the time?

Tennis players very often forget the most important thing in tennis, which is hitting a tennis ball into the court. Then a placement should be added to our shots and only after that we should start worrying about the power.

Never overestimate the power. It looks awesome, but not always it helps to win. You have probably heard that a big amount of the points in a tennis match ends with an unforced error. Latest analysis by ATP reveals that approximately 70% of all points played on the professional tour end with a forced or unforced error. And most of the time player with less errors wins the match…

Trust your instincts

WHY DO TENNIS PLAYERS MAKE UNFORCED ERRORS?

Yes, some of them have big technical weaknesses. Some are too slow with their footwork. However, many players who regularly miss are technically skilled and physically fit for the level they compete. One of the reasons is that tennis players often select wrong and risky shots for the particular situation. However, that is more tactical mistake and we will talk about it later.

Another very common mistake is that tennis players tend to overthink things, especially, technical things. Novak Djokovic once said in one of his interviews that he is his own biggest opponent. What did he mean by that? As a tennis player myself I totally understand what he meant. He meant that sometimes unnecessary thoughts that go through our heads are distracting us from playing our best. Tennis players of different levels very often start thinking about silly technical stuff in the most important moments of the competitive tennis match…

When I was a junior, it happened a lot to me. For example, I played a match in Thailand. A score was 5:4 and 15:30 in the deciding third set. I was about to hit a second serve. We had played for almost three hours and suddenly I started to think about my service grip. Yes, more than ten years of daily practice, thousands of serves hit, no problems with serve or its grip, but at the most inappropriate time I started to question my service grip. And I double faulted… And it is just one example. I have questioned pretty much everything including my ball toss, racket take back on backhand and the way I hold my racket in a ready position… I knew that I had to stop it, but I didn't know how.

Then one day (many years later) I was waiting for the bus in the bus stop. As I was waiting, I was also chewing a gum. A gum ran out of its taste and I decided to throw it out. I saw a little garbage can a few meters away and tried to spit my gum in it. And I made it with the first attempt! Maybe it sounds weird, but it was my ''aha'' moment. I thought to myself: ''I didn't practice in spitting chewing gums before. I had never thought about what shape of the chewing gum I need to create in my mouth before I spit it or how strong I need to spit. I just felt it.

All of us have instincts and muscle memory. Especially, if we do something, for example, play tennis for many years and for uncountable amount of hours. Just trust them!

Many recreational players and even some professional players have a feeling that all of the sudden something has happened to their technique and their technique is different than it used to be a day before. However, the difference is in that mental feeling not in actual technique. Even in the very first tennis practice tennis player develops his unique style. It always stays with him and it cannot be copied or completely changed. Of course, technique can be improved and it should be improved, but that is not the only thing you should think about.

Try to question yourself (better don't) about how often you blink your eyes or how deep you breath in. You can easily mess up that rhythm too, if you overthink it. The bottom line is that most of the tennis players care about their tennis. And more you care about something, more you worry about something. But we can help ourselves to be more productive and successful by just trusting ourselves a little bit more and by not blocking ourselves. As I said before, we all have instincts and muscle memory. So we shouldn't block them. Our bodies know what to do even if it feels weird somedays. On the match court we must trust our instincts and must not think about technique. Sometimes we need those ''aha'' moments to become better. I had mine with the chewing gum.

Watch the ball

WHEN WE UNDERSTAND THAT OUR TECHNIQUE IS GOOD ENOUGH TO COMPETE, WE TRUST IT AND WE DON'T THINK ABOUT IT, WE MUST ACTIVATE OUR BODY BY THE HELP OF EYES AND FEET.

Let's begin with the eyes. You have probably heard your coach saying: "Watch that tennis ball!" But what does it really mean?

You have to watch a tennis ball from the moment your opponent hits it (tennis ball touches the strings of your opponent's racket), till the moment a tennis ball touches the strings of your racket.

Yes, exactly! You must see the contact point. You can see in the pictures that professional tennis players' eyes are still looking at the contact point even the ball is already gone. That happens because it is very important to stay balanced during the shot. If your eyes are focused on the tennis ball at the contact point, it means that you are completely focused and your body is in the balance. However, if you allow your eyes move away from the tennis ball before or even at the moment of an impact, most likely your shoulders, your hips and rest of the body will twitch. And most likely you will make an error or even hit the ball with a frame of the racket. And it doesn't matter which shot.

Whether it is serve, return, forehand, backhand, volley or overhead, you have to see the contact point.

In the reality it is very difficult to keep tracking the tennis ball and see the contact point during the whole rally in the competitive tennis match. However, we should try. And the first step is making sure that we see the contact point for the first shot in the rally either it is serve or return. We can control that. And seeing the contact point actually helps not only focusing and performing cleaner shots, but also trusting your technique. By being focused and reminding yourself about watching the tennis ball, you block your mind from thinking about technical details such as shoulder turn, follow through or anything else. That will help you to be in ″the zone″ and play to your full potential.

Your eyes give a signal to the brain and your brain gives signals to the rest of the body thus letting muscle memory to do its thing.

However, make sure you practice in a right way so that your muscle memory develops correctly…

Move your feet

ALL YOU HAVE TO DO IS STAY FOCUSED, TRUST YOURSELF AND... MOVE YOUR FEET!

You may think: "I know that! Rubbish advice! How can you possibly hit the tennis ball by standing still?" However, by moving your feet I mean that you are really aggressive with your feet, always using a split step before moving to the ball and that you are making little adjustment steps before every stroke to make sure that you are running to the ball and not stretching to it.

Try to make small steps instead of big steps. For example, if you can reach a tennis ball with two steps, make four smaller steps instead. Or, if you can get to the ball with four bigger steps, make six smaller steps instead.

Why? Trust me or not, but in such way you will be able to move faster and run to the ball not stretch to the ball. More adjustment steps mean better balance and more comfortable contact point resulting in fluent and consistent motion.

In my opinion footwork is one of the most underrated aspects of tennis technique. Many coaches tend to look on tennis players' upper body movements and almost ignore the fact that many players are constantly stretching to the ball, not moving sideways when the ball comes straight at them or not moving forward to the shorter ball, in order to attack. Of course, it is possible to play that way, however players with "lazy feet" are missing out on very important aspect of tennis thus not using their full potential.

Nowadays, more often than ever before players in different levels use open stance, especially, on their forehand side. It is, definitely, a good shot to have in your arsenal, especially, in today's modern and fast game when players are constantly pulled out wide off the court. For example, Alexander Zverev, Dominic Thiem, Stefanos Tsitsipas and many other young players have amazing open stance forehands they can hit with a huge power and spin from all around the court. However, we must be careful not to use that open stance because of our laziness. That is very common problem I see among tennis players, especially, recreational tennis players. Lazy open stance in the middle of the court can result in unnecessary error or a pushy shot, which can be easily punished by the opponent. Some experts say that the open stance forehand is today's modern forehand. I partly agree with that because speeds are higher and players have less time to position their bodies sideways and open stance forehand is used more than before. However, I'm a big believer in a neutral stance (not closed stance) when hitting groundstrokes. Willingness to hit in a neutral stance will make you move faster, make small adjustment steps and avoid unnecessary lazy stretching or waiting for the ball. Neutral stance also allows you to be more aggressive by stepping into the court and taking the ball earlier. If the ball is too far away from you, open stance will happen naturally. Just make sure you make those extra steps in all directions, not just when moving sideways, but also when moving forward and backward. By using fast adjustment steps when attacking a short ball, you will be able to significantly take away your opponent's time and make him rush. It is what you want, don't you? And it is also proven that faster you move with your feet, faster your arms move, resulting in higher racket head speed and more powerful stroke.

In my junior career I was fast with my feet, however I used my decent footwork just for chasing "dead" balls while being in defensive situations on the tennis court. I was pretty good at it! However, very often I missed short or slow balls. It happened just because I wasn't adjusting to the ball. I was waiting for the ball to come to me instead of searching that ball with small steps, moving forward and dominate the point by playing faster and more accurate tennis.

It was really interesting how I found out about this imperfection. Once my father took a picture of me hitting a forehand (shame I lost that picture). I was standing on the baseline loading up on my right leg to crush (or frame) an open stance forehand… But the tennis ball in the picture had barely crossed the service line at my side of the court. The ball was a couple of meters away from me and I was standing still hopelessly waiting for the ball to come to me instead of moving forward and finding the ball on my own terms, and hitting it with an accuracy and a power. That was another "aha" moment.

Being aggressive with your feet not only helps hitting better strokes, but also helps mentally as it takes unnecessary nervousness away.

In an interview before the Australian Open women's final a few years ago between Angelique Kerber and Serena Williams, former Wimbledon champion Marion Bartoli highlighted an importance of "moving the feet" for Kerber not only for chasing Serena's powerful groundstrokes, but also for propelling her nervousness away. More active you are with your feet, more confident you become and you loosen up your body.

Clear the net

THE AVERAGE NET CLEARANCE FOR GROUNDSTROKES IN ATP TOUR IS 68 CENTIMETERS.

In this book I'm not focusing on technical details too much, but I can tell you the most important thing in tennis – clear the net. The average net clearance for groundstrokes in ATP tour is 68 centimeters. It is not very low. I would even say that 68 centimeters is pretty high. Some players, for example, Rafael Nadal hits a ball even higher. He and other professionals know the first rule in tennis, which is to hit the ball over the net. Yes, it is the most important thing, followed by hitting the ball inside the court. Simple!

An intention to clear the net will lead you to better technique intuitively. Your groundstrokes will become more fluid with a racket head clearly moving from low to high thus ensuring a topspin. Your volleys and different "feel shots" will become more accurate with a better and more precise follow through. Even your serve will benefit from "clear the net" mindset. Your first serve percentage will increase and the amount of double faults will decrease. Overall, your game will become more consistent.

Consistency and clearing the net can be practiced. One of my favorite drills is called "consistency drill" and it has different variations. For example, you and your practice partner can hit down the middle. As a pair try to keep the ball in play for 40 consecutive times (each player 20 consecutive times) without hitting into the net. Don't be afraid of hitting high over the net. Hitting wide or long is acceptable, if you are able to get the ball back and keep the rally going. This drill can also be performed cross court, down the line or at the net. And you can play around with the numbers. 40 consecutive times is a good start. My personal record with a student is 1000 times.

By using ''consistency drill'', you can also improve your serve consistency. I often try to make 10 second serves (kick or slice) in a row without missing. If I miss, I start from 0.

When I work on my first serves (flat or flat slice), I also try to make 10 serves. But as tennis rules allow us to miss our first serve, I allow myself to hit wide or long, but I don't count it as a serve made. However, hitting into the net still means starting from 0.

I know that concentration, consistency and aggressive footwork requires good physical condition, and there is no shortcut around it.

LET'S DIVE IN FITNESS!

BEING FIT IS IMPORTANT

VERY IMPORTANT THING I NOTICE WHEN OBSERVING A TENNIS PLAYER IS HIS BODILY STRUCTURE AND PHYSICAL ABILITIES SUCH AS STRENGTH, SPEED, ENDURANCE AND FLEXIBILITY.

Tennis is a very tricky sport. In my junior days I had made a lot of mistakes by underestimating opponent just because he is short, skinny or chubby. Yes, of course, athletic bodily type and good physical abilities are very important for successful tennis career, however sometimes good technique, smart tactical play and strong mentality can do wonders. I'm not saying that to set you free from physical training. I'm saying that to make sure you never underestimate an opponent because of any reason. And if you are skinny, grow some muscle. If you are chubby, lose some weight. Shame we can't train height though…

As years go by, even the legends of our sport, for example, John McEnroe, often say that tennis has become more physical comparing to old days.

Professional tennis players spend more time in the gym than ever. Some players at certain stage of the season even spend more time working on their fitness than hitting tennis balls.

Developing physical qualities such as strength, speed, endurance and flexibility on regular basis, are vitally important not just for playing better, but also for staying injury free.

You are what you eat

YES! AS SIMPLE AS THAT.

If you are carrying some unnecessary kilos with you or just don't feel fit, physical activities alone won't help you to lose weight or feel better. In fact, many fitness specialists say that six-pack abs are made in the kitchen…

Sorting out your diet is the fastest way of losing weight, improving general wellbeing and feeling lighter, and faster on the tennis court.

There are just a few simple guidelines I follow. First of all, I pay attention on how much I eat. Many nutritionists recommend eating 2000-2500 calories per day on average. However, calories you consume daily depend on your gender, age, body type, physical activity level and other factors, so I recommend that you find out your own calorie number.

I'm not a massive fan of counting calories, however it is good to have some sort of understanding on how much we need to eat on a daily basis. I know that my goal is to eat somewhere around 3000 calories and drink at least 3 liters of water per day. But bear in mind that I have a pretty active lifestyle. I spend at least five hours per day on the tennis court while coaching plus I practice myself. More active you are, more food and drink you have to consume. For example, Andy Murray used to eat 6000 calories during his off-season training…

Secondly, we need to understand that eating a healthy food means that we can allow ourselves to eat more. Who doesn't like to eat more, right? Most of the times heathy food contains less calories, so we can eat more food without worrying about putting on some extra kilos of fat. For example, I love homemade food and I'm not a big fan of a fast food. I try to avoid products containing a lot of sugar and fat. I stay away from candy and choose chicken or fish instead of pork or lamb. I used to eat fried potatoes, French fries and white bread. But now I'm avoiding them. I choose rise, pasta and grain bread. I love salad. I don't drink soft drinks, but choose water, tea and coffee instead. I don't eat a lot of cakes. I just have a few pieces of a dark chocolate and some fruit with a Greek yogurt for the dessert. That's it! Without torturing myself I weight 80 kilograms and maintain a healthy body fat of approximately 12%.

Warm up

IF YOU ARE A RECREATIONAL TENNIS PLAYER AND YOU DON'T HAVE TIME, OR YOU CAN'T DO FITNESS TRAINING FOR ANY OTHER REASON, MAKE SURE YOU DO AT LEAST A DECENT WARM UP BEFORE PLAYING TENNIS.

Unfortunately, I learnt the importance of taking care of my body quite late... I was in my late teens when I started paying more attention to warming up and cooling down. Well... Before I did some sort of warm up and cool down. I ran a few laps around the court, circled my arms a little bit and stretched my hamstrings for about 15 seconds afterwards. Now I can't imagine my day without proper warm up and cool down. As the old saying goes again: "Better later than never!"

Dynamic warm up is an integral part of any professional tennis player's training day. Firstly, it helps to get your body going and avoid injuries. Secondly, it improves your concentration and mentally prepares you for playing tennis. Thirdly, it is good for your general fitness and wellbeing. Even if you are a recreational tennis player, make sure that you arrive to your tennis practice or match a little bit earlier and you will do a massive favor to your fitness level.

Following warm up exercises are simple and take just 10 minutes. And if you don't know how to perform some of these exercises, feel free to look them up in youtube.com. There are plenty of variations for each exercise, so you can choose your favorite. You can warm up on a tennis court, gym, parking lot or a corridor. These exercises can be done anywhere:

- ✓ Slow jog around the court (one lap);
- ✓ Slow jog around the court with circling wrists in both directions (one lap);
- ✓ Slow jog around the court with circling arms in both directions (one lap);
- ✓ Side step from the baseline to the net and back;
- ✓ Carioca step from the baseline to the net and back;
- ✓ Butt kicks from the baseline to the net and back;
- ✓ High knees from the baseline to the net and back;
- ✓ Groin circles from the baseline to the net and back;
- ✓ Walking calf raises from the baseline to the net;
- ✓ Walking lunges with a twist from the net to the baseline;
- ✓ Short sprint from the baseline to the net.

Once you get your body moving, heart rate up and lower body ready, it is very important to warm up and strengthen your upper body by using a resistance band with 6 simple exercises:

- ✓ Chest pull apart with a resistance band (10 times);
- ✓ Lateral shoulder raise with a resistance band (10 times);

- ✓ Triceps extension with a resistance band (10 times);
- ✓ Biceps curls with a resistance band (10 times);
- ✓ Wrist extension with a resistance band (10 times);
- ✓ Wrist flexion with a resistance band (10 times).

Oh… ***And don't forget to warm up your ankles and a neck!*** 5 slow ankle circles in both directions help to avoid silly ankle injuries. And your neck is involved in every shot in tennis and goes through a lot of hard work while you are playing. Do 5 gentle neck circles in both directions, however make sure that you do this exercise really slow and you are not throwing your head too far back.

Proper warm up is awesome! Personally, for me it not just helps to stay injury free and play better tennis, but also to feel better in my everyday life.

Cool down

ACTUALLY, COOL DOWN IS NOT OPTIONAL. IT IS A MUST DO THING!

It is also really important to cool down and stretch after your tennis practice or match. Firstly, stretching helps preventing injuries and, secondly, it helps your body to recover faster. It is also good for your general wellbeing. Novak Djokovic is a proof that good flexibility helps you to win many titles and stay injury free for a long time.

Below I have written 11 most important passive stretches. Of course, it would be better not to hurry and lay down on a fitness mat for some exercises. However, you can perform all 11 stretches while standing, so cool down can be done in any place after you have played tennis or had any other physical activity.

Hold each stretch for at least 15 seconds and you will be done in approximately 5 minutes:

- ✓ Calf stretch;
- ✓ Hamstring stretch;
- ✓ Quadriceps stretch;
- ✓ Hip flexor stretch;
- ✓ Glute stretch;

- ✓ Lower back stretch;
- ✓ Side stretch;
- ✓ Chest stretch;
- ✓ Shoulder stretch;
- ✓ Wrist flexor stretch;
- ✓ Wrist extensor stretch;

You see… It is not that difficult and time consuming to take care of your body. Just arrive to your tennis session some minutes earlier to warm up, stay a little bit longer to cool down thus improving your tennis fitness and general wellbeing.

Do your cardio

DON'T BELIEVE, IF SOMEONE TRIES TO CONVINCE YOU THAT TENNIS PLAYERS SHOULDN'T RUN LONG DISTANCES.

I agree that tennis players shouldn't look like long distance runners, however look at David Ferrer's fitness routine. He was believed to run massive amount of kilometers daily. Novak Djokovic runs and bikes significant amount of kilometers. Cardio training combined with balanced nutrition and flexibility training is believed to be one of the key aspects of his improved fitness, which propelled him to the top of the ATP ranking list.

Based on my own experience I can tell you that running is a great way not only for improving endurance, but also to lower a heart rate thus enhancing recovery after long and exhausting rallies and matches.

When I was 16 years old, I underwent specific physical test and it showed that my heart rate during physical activities was pretty high. And as a result, I felt tired earlier in the match than I would like to and my recovery for the next match wasn't the best either. So, fitness specialists advised me that I should run more long distances in medium or even slow pace. It was recommended that I should do an aerobic work and run 40 minutes twice per week with the pace of approximately 135-140 heartbeats per minute. In the beginning it felt so slow. Even too slow! I was almost walking, but my fitness coach encouraged me to keep doing it. Before I used to run a lot, however most of the time the speed was too high and I didn't follow the heart rate. I just ran and had an assumption that the faster I run the better it is. Wrong! If you run too fast for too long, your body is going through an anaerobic work (over 150 heartbeats per minute for an average person) and it is impossible to get the necessary energy with just an oxygen. So, body creates energy by using your internal resources and as a result your recovery gets worse and you feel more tired in the long term. So, to lower your heart rate and enhance the recovery, and feel better in general, it is recommended to run long distances in medium or even low pace.

By doing that I felt the progress in a few months' time. I was running in the same 135-140 heart rate zone, however my speed got higher. It means that I had "trained" my heart and improved my aerobic capabilities. My endurance on the tennis court, recovery after long matches and wellness in general improved. By the way, I lost a few unnecessary kilos as well... So, remember when running long distances, faster in not always better. For fast running there are interval trainings, sprints and different agility trainings where high pace is mixed with a low pace or even a rest. That kind of training helps to improve your speed and recovery processes as well.

I recommend you to run for 30 minutes at least once per week with a pace of approximately 135-140 heartbeats per minute. It is awesome, if you run for longer or more often. Keep up a good work! However, there are not that many people who run even once per week on a regular basis. Be that person who runs!

Improve your footwork

LONG DISTANCE RUNNING IS GREAT. BUT IT WON'T DO ALL THE WORK FOR YOU, AS IT WON'T HELP YOUR TENNIS SPECIFIC FOOTWORK ON THE COURT.

To play decent tennis, you must have specific footwork with small steps and the ability to change direction quickly. Also you have to be able to stay on balance while moving forwards, backwards and sideways.

There are many ways for improving your footwork such as cone drills and ladder exercises. They are really awesome and I do those exercises when I'm preparing for the tournaments. However, my favorite way for improving my footwork and being more agile on the tennis court is using a jumping rope. It is so easy to throw a jumping rope in your tennis bag and you can jump almost everywhere because you don't need a massive space to do it.

By jumping regularly, you can achieve a huge improvement in your balance, coordination, speed, quickness, power and overall conditioning. Jumping can also help to condition your forearms, shoulders and the entire core. It also teaches you to be on the toes all the time, which is very good habit to take over to the tennis court.

I recommend you to do a jumping rope workout at least once per week. In my opinion, the most convenient time to do it would be right before your tennis practice as a part of your warm up.

Do at least 1 set of following exercises and it will take approximately 5 minutes of your time:

- ✓ Boxer skip (100 times);
- ✓ Single leg jumps (50 times each leg);
- ✓ Regular bounce (100 times);
- ✓ Feet front to back (50 times);
- ✓ Feet side to side (50 times);
- ✓ Run in place (100 times);
- ✓ Double under (10 times).

Strengthen your body

DON'T BELIEVE THAT TENNIS PLAYERS SHOULDN'T LIFT WEIGHTS AND WORK ON UPPER BODY. YES, TENNIS PLAYERS SHOULDN'T LOOK LIKE SPRINTERS, HOWEVER...

Look at Andy Murray or Rafael Nadal, for example. They both have not only athletic lower bodies, but also very muscular upper bodies.

Strengthening arms and core muscles not only help hitting faster serves and groundstrokes, but it also helps in preventing injuries, which, in my opinion, is the main reason tennis players should be doing upper body workouts.

I'm a living proof of that. During my junior career there was a common opinion that working on the upper body is not recommended and building muscles on arms reduces "feeling" of the tennis ball... So, I didn't do a lot of upper body work. I worked a lot on my lower body though! As a result, I often got injured. And guess where? In my upper body! My elbow, shoulder, wrist, back... Everything used to hurt from time to time. However, since I started working more on my upper body in 2007, I have had a lot less pain in my upper section.

I know… You are busy! Professional tennis players play tennis at least 2-3 hours almost every day. They also work on their fitness for at least 1-2 hours daily and their whole life is devoted to tennis. However, if you are a recreational tennis player playing tennis twice per week, you have other priorities in life as well.

So below I have written a simple and short routine you have to do twice per week. Once per week you can do these 9 exercises right after your tennis practice. And try to find approximately 10 more minutes every week to complete this routine for the second time. For example, after your cardio training.

- ✓ Wall sit (1 minute);
- ✓ Squats (20 times);
- ✓ Calf rises (20 times);
- ✓ Basic plank (1 minute);
- ✓ Crunches (20 times);
- ✓ Supermen (20 times);
- ✓ Plank with both hands on the floor (1 minute);
- ✓ Push-ups (20 times);
- ✓ Bench dips (20 times).

Some of you may think: ''What is it? It is not a real training!'' Well… Good for you! Keep up a good work and forget these 9 simple exercises. I'm happy for you that you pay more attention to your body, however I can name just a few recreational tennis players and not that many wannabe professionals who do at least this kind of training twice per week...

The key to a long-term success is a consistency. Better do less and regularly than a lot and rarely!

Tennis is not a contact sport like basketball or ice hockey, so we don't need a huge muscle mass to push people around, however we need strong deep inner muscles to help body survive regular rotations and impacts when hitting a tennis ball. Yes, we don't need to go through massive weight lifting on a daily basis, but you can lift a little bit, if you want. Weight lifting in moderation will not harm your tennis. However, in general, working with bodyweight, dumbbells and resistance bands combined with a flexibility training is enough.

Keep things simple!

I know that nowadays it is very popular to say that running and other standard fitness methods are not helping our tennis. Some experts say that all fitness drills have to be tennis specific. Yes, I agree that there should be tennis specific exercises. Many of them! However, I'm a big believer that we all must have a strong general physical base. And tennis specific fitness should be added on top of that. In fact, playing tennis itself is tennis specific physical exercise…

LET'S DIVE IN
STRATEGY!

THE BRAIN GAME

WE SHOULD FOCUS NOT ONLY ON PLAYERS' TECHNIQUE AND PHYSICAL ABILITIES, BUT ALSO ON THEIR STRATEGIC AND TACTICAL DECISION MAKING, ESPECIALLY DURING A COMPETITIVE MATCH.

When I travel to tournaments either as a player or as a coach, I often see technically skilled and physically well-built athletes hitting tennis ball so well in their pre-tournament practice sessions. They look unbeatable! And when I was younger, I often fell into that "they look unbeatable" trap and very often overestimated my opponents.

Hitting down the middle, cross court, one up the net and other at the baseline or any other static drill is easier than playing points. Why? Because it takes strategic and tactical thinking away, and it requires more technical and physical effort. During a rally in a competitive tennis match the opposite happens. Player should trust his instincts while moving and hitting, and focus more on what type of shot to choose and where to place that shot, in order to make a life difficult for the opponent. And very often players who have great technique and who can execute practice drills very well, really struggle with a decision making during a match play. On the contrary, some players perform better during a competitive match rather than in a practice session. So don't make any conclusions about your opponents' abilities by just watching them hitting a tennis ball down the middle…

And make sure that you play points regularly during your practice sessions. I play some sort of a point play every day and playing a practice set is one of my favorite things to do.

Focus on your own game

FIRST STAGE OF BECOMING A BETTER MATCH PLAYER IS TO UNDERSTAND YOUR OWN STRATEGY BETTER.

As we clarified before, the majority of tennis points played in all levels end with an error.

Approximately 30% of all points played on a professional tour end with an unforced error. Around 40% of points end with a forced error. It means that the biggest percentage of points played in a professional level end with some sort of error, leaving just 30% for winners as a point ending shot. And it is obvious that most of the time player with less errors wins the match.

So, in my understanding the main goal is to make the ball go over the net and land into the court. Sounds simple or even stupid? Maybe... But just think for a second how often we forget this basic principle. Being reasonably aggressive is important, however big matches and titles are won by playing solid and consistent tennis with the goal to force an error from the opponent, not to hit a winner straight away.

Importance of serving and returning

THE AVERAGE RALLY LENGTH DURING A PROFESSIONAL SINGLES MATCH IN TENNIS IS APPROXIMATELY 4 SHOTS. IT MEANS THAT MOST OF THE TIME EACH PLAYER HITS JUST TWO SHOTS DURING A RALLY AND ONE OF THOSE SHOTS IS EITHER A SERVE OR A RETURN.

Unfortunately, very often two very important elements of tennis are more or less ignored during practice sessions. I'm talking about serving and returning.

In doubles this number is even more dramatic because there are more players on the tennis court and professionals tend to be very aggressive at the net. In doubles 80 % of all rallies are 0 to 4 shots long. In a professional doubles match you won't see many rallies from a baseline, as a big amount of points end with an unreturned serve or a volley hit as the point ending shot by a serving team.

Those numbers show the huge importance of serving and returning. For most of the time rallies are not that long and player with more consistent serve and more reliable return are in a better position to win a match. Those two elements must be practiced regularly, however tennis players very often spend most of the time hitting cross court for hundreds of times and leave just a few minutes for serve practice... And when was the last time you practiced a return of serve?

I suggest everybody to work more not only on a serve and a return, but also on the first shot after a serve and after a return. If you are consistent with your first two shots of the rally, possibility of you winning increases dramatically. For example, practicing a wide serve followed by an offensive shot into the open space is a very good idea. Or practicing a cross court return followed by hitting a defensive shot cross court is a great drill as well.

Of course, it is not all about serving and returning, especially, in a recreational level where people don't serve with the same power and accuracy as professional tennis players. Also, we all love to watch and take part in long and exciting rallies, don't we? So, doing a good old baseline drills are an absolute necessity. Besides, while hitting even down the middle we work on many things such as technique, endurance, concentration and many more.

The lesson from my first professional tournament

JUST DON'T HIT HARDER AS YOU FEEL COMFORTABLE.
UNDERSTANDING YOUR OWN ABILITIES IS THE KEY.

I remember playing my first ITF Futures tournament (the lowest level professional tournament) in my hometown Jurmala when I was 16 years old. An experienced Italian guy crushed me in the first round of the qualifying 6:0 6:2, but that wasn't the main lesson I learnt in that tournament. I was stretching my hamstrings after my embarrassing debut in a professional tennis when my father came to me and said: "I just saw two Spanish guys practicing. They were hitting down the middle for 10 straight minutes with a single tennis ball. And they didn't miss. After 10 minutes one of the guys stopped the rally by catching a tennis ball with his hand and they went to have a quick drink." It felt unbelievable at that time. I thought I was a consistent player, however I couldn't imagine not missing for 10 straight minutes. But now I not only imagine that, but I do that myself. It is not that difficult. Of course, it takes practice. However, the most important thing is not trying to do more than you are capable of doing. Understand your own abilities, use what you have in matches and get better in practice sessions.

The importance of hitting cross court

WHEN WE MAKE SURE THAT THE BALL LANDS INTO THE COURT, THE NEXT STEP IS ACCURACY AND PLACEMENT OF THE TENNIS BALL. MOST COMMONLY USED DIRECTIONS DURING A RALLY ARE CROSS COURT AND DOWN THE LINE.

When you watch professional tennis match, have you ever noticed the huge amount of points when players hit deep balls cross court and play forehand to forehand or backhand to backhand rallies? That is because during a rally the majority of tennis balls are hit cross court as a cross court shot is the ''easiest'' shot in tennis. When I tell that fact to my new students (especially recreational players), their first reaction is: ''Why should I hit at my opponent, if he is standing there? Shouldn't I move him around?'' In an ideal world you should move him around... But only, if you have a chance!

My suggestion is that you should focus more on the incoming tennis ball rather than on your opponent's court positioning. If you receive a deep and difficult ball into the corner from your opponent, just go back cross court, even if you see an open space down the line.

Always try choosing the highest percentage shots and going cross court almost always is a great idea. However, when I say this to my new students, their most common response is: "Really? Why? I want to see my opponent running!" And my answer is: "That's great! But I don't want to see you missing…"

Going down the line

ONE OF THE MOST COMMON CAUSES OF UNFORCED ERRORS IS GOING DOWN THE LINE ON DIFFICULT (DEEP, FAST, ANGLED OR LOW) BALLS.

There is no doubt that it is very important to hit down the line shots, in order to make your opponent move. However, you have to be very careful with your shot selection. I recommend going down the line only when you have enough time to get ready and usually it happens on shorter and slower balls. The whole point of rallying cross court is to wait for that short ball, hit it down the line and put an opponent on the run. And very often that cross court rally will break down because of rushed unforced error. Hopefully, because of your opponent's error…

Cross court vs down the line

YOU SHOULDN'T WAIT FOR YOUR OPPONENT'S ERROR WHILE RALLYING CROSS COURT. YOU SHOULD WAIT FOR SHORTER BALL, GO DOWN THE LINE AND MOVE YOUR OPPONENT AROUND.

But why is it easier to make a successful shot cross court rather than down the line? First of all, there is significantly bigger margin of error. The court is ''bigger'' when going cross court and the ball travels longer distance. If you hit the ball a little bit late, it may go a little bit more to the center of the tennis court, however it will still land into the court. If you are a little bit late on down the line shot, most likely it will go wide into the tram lines.

Secondly, the net is lower in the middle, meaning that it is easier to avoid hitting into the net when you hit cross court because the ball is crossing the net in the middle.

Thirdly, when hitting cross court, you have more time to recover and get ready for the next shot because a tennis ball travels longer distance comparing to down the line shot. Next time you play, when your opponent hits down the line, try replying cross court. That is one of the best ways to counter attack and make your opponent run as he has less time to recover and more court to cover.

When you practice, it is very important to perform drills where you have to move from side to side and change directions of where you hit balls. For example, good old "Figure 8 drill" or "Triangle drill" are awesome for that. And they also are good for better understanding those cross court and down the line shot differences.

I love hitting cross court! It makes me calm on the tennis court knowing that cross court is always the right shot to choose. It may not always be the most effective shot I will win the point straight away, however it is, definitely, the most consistent shot and consistency is the key.

I remember the practice session in Finland where I was playing an international Tennis Europe tournament for 16-year olds. I was practicing with Latvian Ernests Gulbis (former ATP top 10 player) who is just one year younger than me and he was also playing that tournament. That day I was playing badly and I was missing a lot.

During one of the breaks while having a drink, Gulbis said to me: "If you don't "feel the ball" today, just hit cross court. It is much easier!"

To be honest, at that point of my tennis career I wasn't really sure what I was doing on the tennis court tactically. So, I didn't really understand what Ernests meant. At that point I didn't understand these cross court and down the line shot differences I mentioned before. I was mainly playing intuitively, so I didn't listen to him. I didn't understand. And I ended up losing in the first round. Gulbis won that tournament...

When my students finally understand the importance of playing cross court, they very often ask: "What about down the line shots? Are they bad?" No, not at all! As I said before, I doubt that it is possible to win an even tennis match without a single down the line shot. However, you must carefully choose the right moment when to use those shots. As we found out before, when going down the line the court is "smaller", the net is higher and your recovery time for the next shot is shorter.

I recommend going down the line on shorter ball. Shorter ball usually is slower, you have more time to get inside the court and get set with your feet. Thus you also ensure that you are on the attack and that you put your opponent on the run.

However, not every short ball is slow or easy. Sometimes there are short, but fast balls. Sometimes there are short, but really angled balls. So before going down the line make sure that you really have enough time to prepare and get set with your feet.

Accuracy vs power

ANOTHER COMMON MISTAKE WHEN GOING DOWN THE LINE IS ''GOING FOR TOO MUCH''.

Players in different levels, especially, recreational players and juniors try to hit flat winners down the line. Wrong! As we found out before, down the line shot is risky itself. So why should we make it even more risky by hitting it flat and fast?

As we already know, the average net clearance for groundstrokes in ATP tour is 68 centimeters. Yes, lower doesn't mean better. Lower means more risk and less time to recover for you, and more comfort for your opponent. Even if you make that flat shot and you don't get that lucky winner, it will be in your opponent's comfort zone right about in his waist height. Many great coaches suggest that we should try to hit with a topspin and well above the net that the ball after a bounce jumps up and leaves your opponent's comfort zone. Think about it and try it out next time. Personally, for me it is easier to return a flat ball in a waist level, rather than high and deep ball with more topspin.

There are many ways how to force our opponent to make an error. It is not all about the power. We can use different spins, move our opponent around and play to his weaknesses. Tennis is an interesting game, so don't turn it in ''who wants to hit harder'' competition.

Understand your own game

THE KEY OF SUCCESS IN TENNIS IS UNDERSTANDING YOUR OWN ABILITIES AND HAVE COMPLETE FEEL AND CONTROL OVER YOUR SHOTS.

I recommend my students to hit as strong as they feel comfortable. I encourage everybody to be sure that their technique is correct and that their shots will land into the court. It is all about hitting free and fluent shots. There is no need to constantly worry about the power of your shots and waste an energy by bashing a tennis ball with wrong technique thus risking to make cheap errors.

You can't be 100 percent certain about anything in life, so I suggest hitting with 90 percent certainty that your shot will go over the net and land into the court.

I teach my students that it is not all about the power. If they do everything correctly, their shots will become stronger intuitively as time goes by. This understanding brought myself a massive success.

Take a look at Gilles Simon, for example. In my opinion he is one of the smartest players there has ever been on the professional tour. And not just in a way he outsmarts his opponents, but also in a way how well he understands his own game, his strengths, his weaknesses and his technical abilities. I rarely see him doing something silly during the match. He is not the tallest and most powerful guy on the ATP tour, however he fully understands his abilities and he is not trying to do more than he can and more than he is sure that he can do on the match court. Yes, his shots are not as powerful as Federer's, for example. But who cares? He has beaten Federer purely by holding on to his game plan from the first to the last point of the match. He didn't look worried about the fact that Federer was dominating rallies and hitting more winners. He held on to his patient game, hit his shots with control and didn't go for too much power focusing on the placement instead.

The same story applies to, for example, Simona Halep and Caroline Wozniacki on the women's side. If we measured average shot speed, they wouldn't be even close to number one in the world ranking and winning Grand Slams...

I'm trying to say that too many tennis players even in the highest level lose matches. Yes, they lose matches rather than their opponents win.

They often try to play too aggressive, go for too much and "over hit" their shots. As we found out before, they make too much unforced errors, because they often can't resist the temptation to finish rally early. Sometimes it also happens that players can't take it physically anymore, so they go for too much risk to stop torturing themselves, but that is a poor excuse. As I said in the beginning, sport is tough. And we should enjoy it.

Understanding your own game, accepting your technical abilities and sticking to your game plan is an amazing skill. For example, David Ferrer was so good at it. I call it a mental skill and it requires a lot of determination, and pretty high tennis IQ as well. Doing what you do the best and trusting your strengths in the crucial stages of the match often determine the winner.

Of course, we all should work on our games and try to get better and hit harder with more accuracy. However, that should be done in the practice sessions. During a match we should use what we have and what we feel confident about.

Have a game plan

IT ALL MAY SOUND SIMPLE, HOWEVER BEING CALM UNDER THE PRESSURE AND TRUSTING YOUR GAME PLAN IS NOT EASY.

I know that. I have been there in my junior days, as I didn't have a clear vision on how I wanted to structure my own point. And if you don't have a clear game plan, most likely you will be more nervous and impatient during a competitive tennis match.

Probably, by now you may be thinking: ''Oh no... This guy teaches us grinding cross court, running from side to side all the time, occasionally hitting down the line and waiting for the opponent to make a mistake...'' Yes, I do believe that you will have to run, because tennis is a sport and you are supposed to be running and sweating when doing sports. Yes, I do believe that most of the time when playing from the baseline you should hit cross court, because of the court geometry and your recovery time. Yes, I would characterize myself as a counter puncher, if we talk about my playing style. I spend quite a lot of time defending and playing from a baseline while waiting for the right ball to attack. But my game is not about waiting for the opponent's error. It is all about building the point.

By the way, my favorite player while growing up was a former world number one and a Grand Slam champion Lleyton Hewitt. I loved his fighting spirit and his playing style. He is one of the best counter punchers a tennis world has ever seen, so I learnt a lot by watching Lleyton's matches on TV and I was quite sad when he retired…

My perfect point

I HAVE A CLEAR MIND BEFORE EVERY POINT AND I ALWAYS KNOW WHAT I WANT TO ACHIEVE DURING THAT PARTICULAR POINT.

For example, when I serve, I love to go wide with my first serve thus pushing my opponent off the court and creating an open space where to hit my next shot, if I have a chance. When I return a serve, my main goal is just to get the ball over the net and into the court. Return is a very difficult shot, so most of the time I aim my return cross court as it is the easiest and safest shot direction.

As you already know, the majority of points end within four shots. However, I'm ready to go as long as it takes to win a point. Actually, I really enjoy long rallies. If my serve has been neutralized or I have successfully returned my opponent's serve, and neutral rally begins, I start building the point by hitting cross court. I wait for that slower ball to go down the line and make my opponent run. While being on the run, it is very likely that he will reply even shorter (probably somewhere around service line). If he doesn't reply short or slow, I don't worry. I build by playing cross court again and wait for the next opportunity to go down the line. However, if he replies really short after my down the line shot, that is what I'm actually waiting for. I move up to that short ball and make an accurate approach shot to my opponent's backhand or into the open court. Then I position myself at the net and try to finish the rally with an accurate volley or an overhead into the open space.

This is the mindset I have before starting every point in tennis match. A clear picture of what I want to achieve gives me peace and makes me calm on the tennis court, and helps me to concentrate.

As you see, I'm a big fan of all court tennis. However, very often points break down during the "building process" as we make aces, commit double faults, hit winners and make errors. In fact, there are matches where I get a chance to hit just a couple of volleys, if my opponent is extremely aggressive and makes me to defend a lot. But I always have my game plan in my mind before every point and I stick to it no matter what.

Divide court into zones

TO BETTER UNDERSTAND MY TACTICAL APPROACH, I HAVE DIVIDED THE TENNIS COURT INTO 4 ZONES. FROM EVERY ZONE THERE ARE CERTAIN PATTERNS WHERE I SUGGEST TO HIT THE TENNIS BALL.

Zone 1

If the ball bounces into the zone 1 (highlighted area on the baseline), most of the time I go back cross court and wait for the shorter ball to start moving my opponent around.

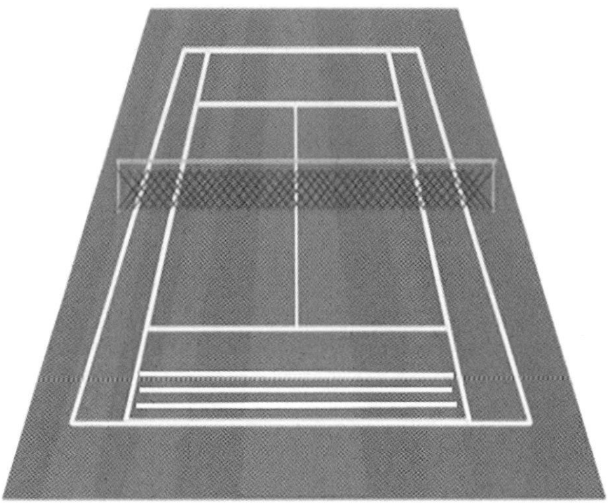

Zone 2

If the ball bounces into the zone 2 (highlighted area in the mid-court), I try to go down the line and move my opponent around.

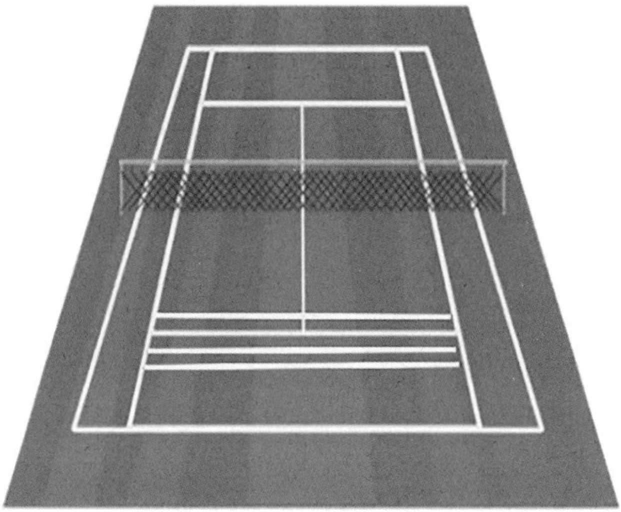

Zone 3

If the ball bounces in the zone 3 (highlighted area in the service box), I usually hit an approach shot to the opponent's backhand or into the open court and go to the net.

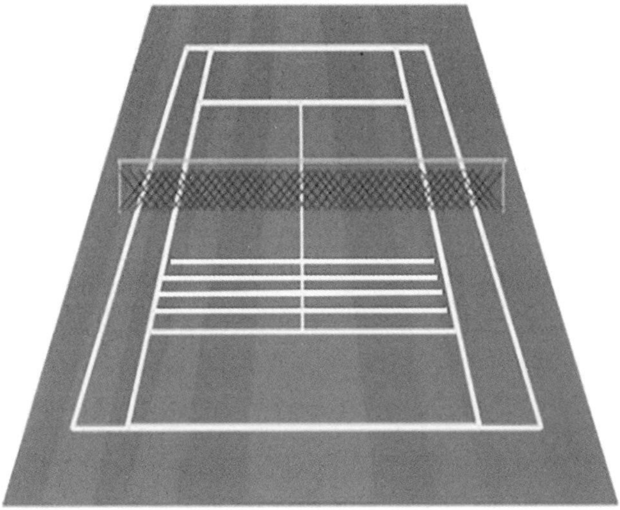

Zone 4

After the approach shot, I position myself at the net in the zone 4 (highlighted area close to the net). From there I either hit either a volley or an overhead into the open space.

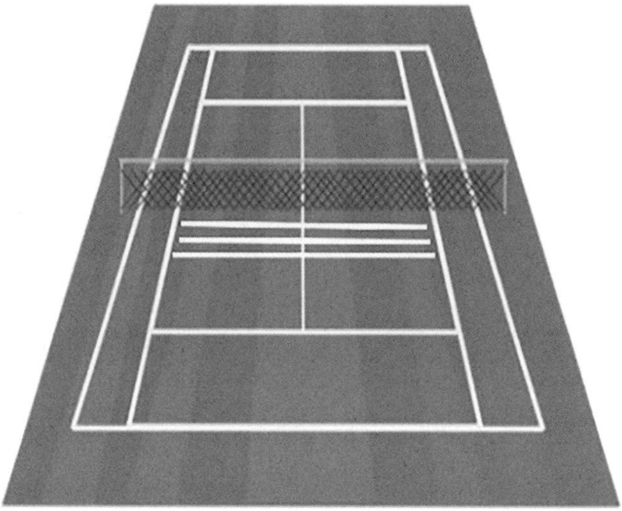

In my opinion, coming to the net is a great way to keep an offensive mindset throughout a match, put a pressure on your opponent and win more points in an aggressive manner without taking a big risk. Actually, I would love to see tennis players coming to the net more during the matches and spending more time at the net while practicing volleys and approach shots in their practice sessions.

Of course, there may be some exceptions to my game plan. For example, the mid-court ball bouncing into zone 2 can be low and fast making it impossible to go down the line. Then I hit it back cross court. But the bottom line is that I have a plan in my head and my shot placement depends more on the incoming tennis ball rather than on my opponent's court positioning.

Stick to your A game

IT IS VERY IMPORTANT TO STICK TO YOUR GAME PLAN OR, AS I CALL IT, YOUR A GAME.

Sometimes we all have some distractions such as a wind, a sun, an opponent playing well or something else. But it is very important to stick to your A game as long as possible. I'm not saying that my strategy explained before is the only possible way how to structure a point. It is my favorite way of playing tennis and I teach it to my students. I believe that it is the very rational and effective game plan and you can't go wrong playing this way. However, you might have different strengths in your game. You just need to know them and create your own game plan highlighting those strengths.

Maybe you are a serve and volley player with an awesome volley and exquisite touch. Good! Maybe you are an ultimate grinder from the baseline who rarely misses and is able to run for hours. Good! Or maybe you are an aggressive baseliner loving to dominate the rallies with your powerful forehand. Good! The bottom line is that you must have your A game and you have to stick to it.

I know that this may sound a little bit boring. But have you heard an old saying stating that all great things are simple? That is what I'm trying to say!

Back in my junior days I used to have matches when I over prepared and created several game plans, but got confused in my tactical decisions by jumping from one plan to another thus letting an unnecessary errors creep in my game. I used to think: ''Well... This guy has really extreme forehand grip. I bet he doesn't like low balls, so I need to slice to his forehand a lot.'' Or:'' I must make a lot of drop shots! This guy is very slow...'' Actually, there is nothing wrong with these tactics. These little things are good for mixing things up during a match, however, you can't do them too often. And I was doing a lot of unnecessary thing too often. The problem was that being so creative wasn't my A game. It wasn't my basic strategy. Actually, I didn't know what was my basic strategy back then. With those different little tactics I, probably, broke down my opponents' game a little bit, but I made even more damage to my own game. I started questioning my strokes, made weird decisions, missed too much and I didn't have a vision on how to play the most important points in the match. I over complicated things.

Of course, I make small tactical adjustments depending on who my opponent is. For example, if I play lefty, I change my second serve placement. As the majority of people are right handed, most of the time

I serve kick serve and it jumps up high to the returner's backhand, and it is great. But, if I play against left hander, my kick serve goes straight into his forehand, which is the strength for most of the tennis players. So, against lefties I change my primary tactics and serve a heavy slice serve to their backhand.

Quite often tennis players have much weaker backhand comparing to their forehand. In that case, I try to use my opponent's weakness and address more balls there. For example, if I play a righty, I go down the line with my forehand a little more than I normally would against a player with a decent backhand. And, contrary, I go down the line with my backhand more, if I play a lefty with a weak backhand.

As you see, I'm not saying that you shouldn't adapt your strategy to your opponent. You can change small tactical details, but your general strategy should remain the same and you should stick to your A game. There are some professional tennis players who don't change their strategy at all. Some players change it a little bit, but most of them make small adjustments and mainly rely on their strengths.

In one of his many interviews, Roger Federer once said that he focuses 80 percent on his regular game plan and maximum 20 percent are changed depending on who is his opponent and what are his strengths and weaknesses.

Tennis is difficult itself. Playing under physical and mental pressure, and hitting that small yellow ball while running is not an easy thing to do. So, let's keep things simple, play mainly with our strengths and worry about our opponents' weaknesses later.

Playing a tennis match is similar to living a life. Focusing on the path that we have chosen and relaying on our strengths can lead to a massive success.

LET'S DIVE IN PSYCHOLOGY!

IT IS ALL IN YOUR MIND

I LOVE ''THE BRAIN PART'' OF TENNIS. I LOVE TEACHING TACTICAL AND MENTAL GAME OF TENNIS, BECAUSE I BELIEVE THAT IT TAKES JUST AN UNDERSTANDING AND YOU CAN TAKE YOUR GAME TO THE NEXT LEVEL WITH THE TECHNICAL AND PHYSICAL QUALITIES YOU ALREADY HAVE.

Tennis, the same as majority of other sports, is divided in four main aspects – technical, physical, tactical and mental. And, unfortunately, mental aspect of tennis is often the less discussed and taught aspect of all. Just imagine typical practice session with a tennis coach and most likely that at least 80 % of that practice are devoted to technical instruction, 15 % to some tactical details and maybe 5 % are devoted to mental development. And most of the time mental development sounds like: ''C'mon! You can do it! Don't give up and push yourself!'' I hope you have a good coach and you get more significant mental development, however that is my own experience I got as a junior tennis player.

To be honest, I wasn't very ''mental'' coach in the beginning of my coaching career. I just didn't know what to say. Now it is a complete opposite. I have matured as a person and as a tennis professional. I have worked with myself a lot by doing independent studies and putting everything into practice in my own game, and I have been lucky to be able to work together with amazing tennis coaches in recent years.

I have proved to myself that my mental approach works. It works for my students and it works for me, as I'm playing the best tennis of my life in my thirties and I'm beating full time professional tennis players who are more than 10 years younger and technically better than me. And the same happens with my students. They play the best tennis of their lives. And not because they have better looking technique…

Tennis is just a game

IT ALL BEGINS WITH AN UNDERSTANDING THAT TENNIS IS A GAME. AND GAMES ARE SUPPOSED TO BE FUN. WHETHER IT IS A BOARD GAME, XBOX OR TENNIS MATCH, IT IS STILL A GAME AND IT IS SUPPOSED TO BE FUN AND WE SHOULD ENJOY IT.

It may sound weird, but I started enjoying tennis when I was already 21 years old. It wasn't like I didn't enjoy it before, however I didn't have so much passion for the game as I have now. By that time, I had achieved quite a lot. I had pretty successful junior career. I also won national championship and represented my country in Davis Cup. However, I took tennis for granted. Maybe because my family funded it for me…

Very often the world's best tennis players such as Roger Federer and Novak Djokovic emphasize the importance of enjoying the game even there are big titles and millions of dollars on stake.

As the time went by, I started making my own money for living by coaching more serious. As I started coaching more serious, I had to help more students and solve more problems. So I started to learn tennis deeper. I needed more information. I understood that learning should never stop and we never know enough. In addition to learning by watching and analyzing professional players, exchanging opinions with other coaches and attending conferences and seminars, I devoted a lot of time to the online learning. And it worked. I learnt a lot online. I still do.

Before teaching anything to anyone I always try it out myself first. Getting better in coaching is a never ending process and for me this process leads to enjoying tennis more and more each day. If you play tennis and you are still reading this, I'm sure that you enjoy this game too.

Being nervous is okay

IF YOU GET TOO NERVOUS IN THE MORNING BEFORE AN IMPORTANT TENNIS MATCH, YOU HAVE TO REMEMBER THAT TENNIS IS JUST A GAME.

Very important game though… And in fact, it is normal to get nervous. More you care about something, more nervous you get. It is understandable. And it is not just in tennis. It is everywhere in life. And it is okay. However, we can't let nervousness and stress beat us. We must overcome it and that is why sport is great as it builds our characters. As tennis legend Andre Agassi once said: ''Tennis prepares you for life!''

Don't worry! Nerves are normal. However, there are different types of stress. Distress means negative stress when person can't adapt to the stressor, whereas eustress is beneficial and even motivational stress. I believe that every athlete who has a passion for the sport goes through some sort of stress before the match. Many tennis players admit that they are nervous, but they don't worry about that. They even find a little bit of stress motivational.

Experienced *Venus Williams once said "Nerves are normal. You can't be cured from them unless you are a machine. It is all about how you deal with it and how you overcome that moment."*

I have struggled with my nerves as well, especially, during my junior career. However, I have always looked calm on the tennis court. Everyone always thought that I'm mentally very strong. I rarely talked to myself or broke rackets. I rarely showed negative emotions. I was really withheld. I have never been really bad mentally, however I always felt that I could get better. The biggest problem for me was a pre-match nervousness. I knew I had practiced regularly and worked on my fitness as well, and I really enjoyed tennis, but I was too nervous. And the biggest mistake I made when trying to calm myself down was thinking that there is something wrong with me getting nervous. I often said to myself: "C'mon, calm down! What is wrong with you? It is going to be alright. Just play!" But it didn't work. I thought that other players are calm and it is just me worrying. I dreamt to play without any stress and doubts. However, as I started to study tennis deeper, I understood that being nervous is okay. I understood that everybody gets nervous and nervousness actually motivates us. Nervousness means that we care. More we worry about the fact that we are nervous and try not to worry, more nervous and anxious we get. So, I started to accept that little stress and nervousness, and took that positive energy out of it. Now I really accept it. In fact, I believe that without a positive stress it is impossible to be successful. Many athletes in different sports would agree with me that, if the pre-match nervousness is completely gone, most likely the passion for the game is gone as well and without the passion it is difficult to enjoy the sport and almost impossible to win big titles and important matches in any level. We should enjoy the game, accept that we are getting nervous, not think about it and focus on the process rather than on the outcome.

Be positive

YES! AS SIMPLY AS THAT. BE POSITIVE!

Being positive and optimistic is very crucial factor for success in tennis (and in life). Our mindset very often is responsible for the outcome of things we do.

Human psychology is simple. It all starts with a thought. Our thoughts and attitude create our emotions and feelings thus influencing our behavior and results.

Focus on the process

BEFORE THE MATCH WE TEND TO PUT TOO MUCH PRESSURE ON OURSELVES BY THINKING ABOUT THE OUTCOME OF THE MATCH AND TOO OFTEN WE DOUBT IN OURSELVES…

Have you ever thought that the opponent you are going to face is too tough to beat? I have…

Sometimes we underestimate our opponents. Have you ever had a match when you were too confident going in? And as the match progressed the result wasn't going in your favor and in the end you lost to, as you thought, ''weaker'' opponent? I have had such matches…

Luckily for me it is the thing of the past. I have learnt to focus on the process rather than on the outcome. And these mental changes are responsible for achieving my best results in my late twenties. I haven't started to hit the ball harder or run faster. I'm just mentally stronger. I believe in myself more.

It is really important to realize that you are unique. You are YOU! You are the one and only. You are in the center of your own life. You dictate your life. You wake up in the morning, think with your brain, see with your eyes and make your decisions. I bet you have something unique that even Roger Federer doesn't have. If someone can make a difference in your life, then it is you.

In tennis (and in life), you have to believe that you are the best just because you are you. There is no point in thinking that you are worse in doing something than someone. Forget it! Even if you are weaker player "on paper" than your next opponent who has achieved more in tennis or beaten you before… Just forget it! Being too realistic and staying in your comfort zone won't help you to get better. You have to be a little bit crazy to be successful in any profession or even any hobby. You have to set your goals higher than realistic.

You can beat anybody

IN TENNIS YOU HAVE TO BELIEVE THAT YOU CAN BEAT ANYBODY. YES, ANYBODY!

Too often people lose matches they can win just because they don't believe in themselves. That is sad! I often hear people saying: ''I don't know... He is too good... He is practicing more and I don't think I can beat him...'' Or even worse: ''Tomorrow I play a guy I have never seen playing, but I saw his ranking. He must be so good! I will be happy just to win a few games...'' I normally don't hate things and I'm very reserved, however, when I hear someone saying these things I want to bang my head against the wall. Of course, I have never done that. I remain calm and start explaining my point of view to my students.

Okay, I understand! We all are human beings and such thoughts may come in our minds. It is the same as I talked before about the stress and nervousness. However, you shouldn't say it out loud. And whenever these thoughts mess up with your mind before a tennis match, just trick your mind by saying to yourself: ''I'm the best! I can beat anybody!'' And by anybody, I mean ANYBODY.

As weird as it may sound, you must believe that you can beat even Federer or Williams.

When I say this to my students for the first time, they most likely start smiling and say: "Ha ha! Sure coach..." Some of them may think that I'm a little bit crazy, but I don't care. It works! Only by setting high goals you can achieve your "realistic" goals.

Only by setting high goals you can really get better. If there were no "crazy" people setting unrealistic goals, probably, we would still be playing tennis with wooden rackets, there were no airplanes and the Internet would only be in our dreams. Being too realistic limits you. People shouldn't be afraid to fail. People should be afraid of not trying. Dreaming big is exciting!

In that tournament where I got my ATP ranking point for the first time, I was the second oldest player in the main draw. Practicing and travelling to professional tournaments is not the most profitable thing to do for me, however, I really enjoy competing, preparing for the tournaments and it helps in my coaching job as well, as I can share a practical experience with my students. A lot of guys I used to practice and compete together started coaching straight after graduating from college or even earlier. They stopped their playing careers and devoted themselves hundred percent to the coaching. That is okay. I totally get it. However, some of the guys often ask me: ''Why? Why are you doing this? Spending all that money? Why are you still torturing yourself in those early morning practice sessions and tough matches competing with younger guys? Why don't you just come down and stick to the coaching?'' The answer is easy. It just comes from my heart. I can't imagine living my life without hard practice sessions and competing in tennis tournaments. It has always been my lifestyle. I really enjoy the game. And I hope that it will remain this way.

But it was tough in the past. I slightly hated myself for not being able to achieve ATP ranking. That was my goal for more than a decade. I often tried to fool myself in different ways by saying that I have achieved a lot. However, I couldn't fool myself. I wanted it so bad even I was almost 30 years old. And it drove me crazy. I wasn't sure that things I have been teaching to my students were really working as I test everything on myself and I hadn't achieved my goal…

However, now when I have achieved my goal, I'm still hungry for more success. I still enjoy the game. I still want to compete and achieve even more. And I want to share my knowledge and passion with you. I want you to dream big. I want you to set your goal high, work hard to achieve that goal and most importantly enjoy the process. I want you to always believe that you can win no matter whom you face.

Venus Williams once said: "You have to believe in yourself when no one else does. That makes you a winner right there. In my mind I'm always the best. If I walk out on the court and think that other person is better, I have already lost."

That's right! Before any tennis match you have to convince yourself that you are the best and you can win. You have to be in that "beast" mode. You have to be in "the zone".

Being in "the zone"

EVEN IF YOU ARE A RECREATIONAL TENNIS PLAYER AND PRACTICE JUST ONCE PER WEEK, YOU HAVE ALL THE NECESSARY TECHNICAL SKILLS AND PHYSICAL ABILITIES FOR COMPETING AGAINST OTHER PLAYERS, YOU HAVE TO FIND A WAY HOW TO GET IN YOUR ''ZONE''.

I describe "the zone" as the state of mind when your mind is free from unnecessary and disturbing thoughts, you feel confident and ready to play your best tennis, and you completely believe your game plan for the upcoming match. You are positively nervous and you can't wait to step on the tennis court. You are eager to compete and ready to enjoy the game.

These simple tips have helped some of my students and many other tennis players from different countries. However, some of them still struggle to be hundred percent in "the zone". They believe in themselves, they enjoy the game and they want to compete, however their mind still drifts away at the most inconvenient time. And most of the time thoughts about the outcome (most likely losing) come in their mind. In fact, there is a massive difference between loving to win and hating to lose. I think loving to win is better. It is healthier from mental perspective. It is motivating, whereas not wanting to lose or even being afraid to lose makes you too nervous and too tight. Not wanting to lose is not working.

Big turning point for me was reading a quote from Roger Federer: "I really enjoy winning, where as many other guys hate losing."

It may sound simple, however many of us are trapped in that "I hate losing" mindset and put too much pressure on the outcome of the match. As I mentioned earlier, you should focus on the process, rather than on the outcome. Yes, you must believe that you can win. You should even visualize yourself winning. And remind yourself that you can win every time when that stupid and scary thought about losing comes into your mind. And when you are in the winning mindset, all you need to do is to focus on the process.

You should focus on doing your best. That's all you are really able to control - your own decisions and actions. Unfortunately, you can't control winning. You have to be confident about yourself and believe that you can win, however you can't control it. You can control the process. And when you are fully focused on the process, you have no time to think about the outcome. You just try to do your best and competitive tennis turns out to be fun. That massive nervousness disappears and it is easier to remain positive even after loses.

You can learn more from a loss than from a victory.
I believe that I never lose. I believe that I either win or learn…

I don't remember exact date and time (somewhere around 2011) when I understood that focusing on the process rather than on the outcome is the key, but I do remember that this revelation changed my approach to tennis. That was another "aha" moment. That "aha" moment came from studying many professional tennis players' case studies and interviews. While I lived in Scotland and I had a free time from studying, practicing and competing, I spent hours and hours on searching for different kind of tennis related information online. I searched mainly for tactical and mental information. I watched thousands of videos with professional tennis players competing and made notes on strategy, and tactics they use against each other, and tried to implement them into my game. I remember that there was a time, when I had a feeling that I have seen every tennis related YouTube video…

I also read autobiographies, scientific papers and simple interviews with the world's best athletes (not only tennis players). The more I read that stuff, the more one particular topic kept coming up.

Many famous athletes constantly mentioned that focusing on the process is the key. They said that they don't think about the result. They believe that they can win, but all they focus on is the process and they just want to do their best.

At first it sounded to me like simple and automatic phrases of politeness that they say in every interview. However, when I dug deeper and started to implement this approach myself, I understood that these are not phrases of politeness. These are phrases of success. Of course, it may take time to fully accept, understand and engage in that "focusing on the process" mindset, however it is worth it. In the beginning telling yourself to focus on the process may feel artificial, however as the times goes by and you keep focusing on the process, it becomes a habit and you can really enjoy the game and play fearless tennis with a free mind.

When I started to implement this approach myself, it wasn't easy. But now I have reached the state of mind where I truly focus on the process during the match play. I have almost no pressure about the outcome of the match. In fact, I have reached the state of mind that I don't care whom I play against. Yes, I need to know my opponent, his playing style, his strengths and weaknesses, however I don't care what is his ranking and I don't care about his previous achievements. Now I can mainly focus on executing my game plan. And I don't care, whether my opponent is Novak Djokovic, some guy ranked 500 in ATP ranking or some club player who plays tennis twice per week as a hobby. We all are human beings and I try not to overestimate or underestimate tennis players. This way it is easier not only to play your best tennis and win matches. This way it is also easier to accept losing and move forward.

Losing is tough. No one likes to lose. Me neither. And it is normal because we all want to be successful. But in order to be successful, we need to lose with the respect. We need to respect our own tennis and our opponent's tennis as well. That is the only way we can get better and learn something from the loss. In fact, it is often easier to learn from a loss than a win. Winning sometimes blurs our minds. And losing frustrates us way too much. In an ideal world we should treat winning and losing the same way. Of course, after a win we are happier. I'm not asking you to be happy after a loss. However, after the match, when the emotions have come down, it is crucial to analyze your performance and the process rather than the outcome. Maybe you played not your best match, but managed to win. Or maybe you played a good match and the opponent was just better that day. After every match you have to assess your performance. And that is the only way to get better.

I don't care who is my opponent. I respect everybody, but I'm afraid of nobody.

Before stepping out on the match court, I entirely focus on the process and I don't care, if I would have to face Roger Federer at his best or some hobby player, who practices twice per week. I'm confident that I can win. But my focus is on the process. I'm happy for the victory, but I'm ready to accept defeat. After the match I assess my performance and move forward. There is no time for a massive celebration or a big sadness. A few smiles or a couple of tears is enough. We don't need that roller coaster ride. We need stability.

As the old saying goes: "Sportsmanship is when a guy walks off the court and you can't tell whether he won or lost, because he carries himself with pride and respect."

One point at time

DO YOU KNOW BUSINESS MAGNATE RICHARD BRANSON? IN ONE OF THE INTERVIEWS HE SAID THAT THE BIGGEST LESSON HE HAS LEARNT IN TENNIS IS TO TREAT EACH POINT SEPARATELY. AND HE SAYS THAT THIS LESSON HELPS HIM IN LIFE AND BUSINESS AS WELL.

It is quite simple. Point becomes game. Game becomes set. Set becomes match. Match becomes tournament. Tournament becomes season. Season becomes career…

Do you understand what I mean? I mean that you have to stay positive and play one point at time because that one point is all what matters at that moment. That one point can make a huge difference. And it doesn't matter who is your opponent or what is the score.

Very often tennis players of different levels think too far ahead. They think that their opponent is too tough to beat. They think that being 2:5 down in the deciding set is a disaster. Sometimes life gets in a way and some players start wondering about personal things. But we all have to learn to enjoy every moment we spend on tennis court. Every moment and every point can be a changing point not only in one particular match, but also in a whole career.

I'm sorry to tell you, but most likely you will lose points during a tennis match. Even the world's best tennis players win only approximately 55% of all points played during the season. It means that it is normal to lose almost every second point. The main things are to stay positive, accept that, focus on the next point and make the right decisions when it matters.

In my opinion, Rafael Nadal is amazing in playing one point at time. It is very hard to tell what is the score when he plays by just a looking at him. His facial and body languages rarely change, and he treats himself very similarly in both – victory or defeat.

Rafael Nadal once said :"I play each point like my life depends on it."

Just go for it

THE KEY FOR SUCCESS IN ANY ASPECT OF LIFE IS PRACTICE.

Information in this book requires practice as well. And most of this information should be practiced in match situations. It may take some time until all rules seem natural to you and become automatic, however, it is worth trying. Because you want to enjoy tennis, play and compete with positive, and free mind, don't you?

Competing is very important in every sport. To some extent it is the most important part of sport. Tennis is not an exception. I know many players of different levels who fear competing because they are scared of losing. But there is nothing wrong with losing. Losing is a part of the road to the victory. Even professional tennis players lose almost every week, because there is only one winner in the tournament.

Being scared of losing is something we all should get rid of. Being scared of losing should be replaced with being eager to win. Many successful athletes (and not only athletes) say that a big reason for their success is that they have failed over and over again in their lives. But they didn't stop. They kept going for it.

Stan Wawrinka's tattoo, quoting the famous novelist Samuel Beckett, says it all: "Ever tried. Ever failed. No matter. Try again. Fail again. Fail better."

I DON'T CARE WHO IS MY OPPONENT. I RESPECT EVERYBODY, BUT I'M AFRAID OF NOBODY.

MAXIMIZE YOUR TENNIS POTENTIAL

Rihards Emulins

ABOUT THE AUTHOR

Rihards Emulins is a certified tennis coach, professional tennis player, tennis lover and founder of webtennistraining.com. Rihards is involved in tennis for more than 20 years, achieved ATP ranking, represented Latvia in Davis Cup, won National Championship and BUCS (British Universities and Colleges Sport) team championship as a proud member of University of Stirling men's tennis team. Tennis is something Rihards knows the best and he can talk about this sport endlessly. He has worked with tennis players of different levels and his training methods have already helped thousands of players to take their games to the next level.